Exploring
Perspective Hand Drawing
Fundamentals for Interior Design

Activity Sketch Book

Stephanie M. Sipp

PUBLICATIONS

Schroff Development Corporation

www.SDCpublications.com

Schroff Development Corporation
P.O. Box 1334
Mission KS 66222
(913) 262-2664
www.SDCpublications.com

Publisher: Stephen Schroff

Copyright © 2012 by Stephanie M. Sipp

All rights reserved. This document may not be copied, photocopied, reproduced, transmitted, or translated in any form or for any purpose without the express written consent of the publisher, Schroff Development Corporation.

IT IS A VIOLATION OF UNITED STATES COPYRIGHT LAWS TO MAKE COPIES IN ANY FORM OR MEDIA OF THE CONTENTS OF THIS BOOK FOR EITHER COMMERCIAL OR EDUCATIONAL PURPOSES WITHOUT EXPRESS WRITTEN PERMISSION.

Examination Copies:

Books received as examination copies are for review purposes only and may not be made available for student use. Resale of examination copies is prohibited.

Electronic Files:

Any electronic files associated with this book are licensed to the original user only. These files may not be transferred to any other party.

Contents

PREFACE		**5**
ORIENTATION		**7**
ACTIVITY 1.1	DRAWING CONSISTENT LINES	9
ACTIVITY 1.2	LINES WITH WEIGHT VARIATION	11
ACTIVITY 1.3	SQUARE BOXES WITH LINES	13
ACTIVITY 1.4	MORE PRACTICE WITH LINES AND SHAPES	15
THE BOX		**17**
ACTIVITY 2.1	ONE-POINT PERSPECTIVE VIEWS	19
ACTIVITY 2.2	ONE-POINT PERSPECTIVE BOXES	21
ACTIVITY 2.3	MORE ONE-POINT PERSPECTIVE BOXES	23
ACTIVITY 2.4	FREE HAND ONE-POINT PERSPECTIVE BOXES	27
ACTIVITY 2.5	OBJECTS IN ONE-POINT PERSPECTIVE	29
ACTIVITY 2.6	TWO-POINT PERSPECTIVE BOX	31
ACTIVITY 2.7	BOXES FROM DIFFERENT VIEWPOINTS	35
ACTIVITY 2.8	FREE HAND TWO-POINT PERSPECTIVE DRAWINGS	35
ACTIVITY 2.9	MULTIVIEW DRAWINGS OF OBJECTS	37
ACTIVITY 2.10	MULTIVIEW DRAWINGS OF SHAPES	39
ACTIVITY 2.11	VISUALIZING THREE DIMENSIONAL OBJECTS	45
ACTIVITY 2.12	FINDING PROPORTION WITH A GRID	47
ACTIVITY 2.13	DRAWING A SOFA WITH A GRID	49
ACTIVITY 2.14	PROPOTION IN PERSPECTIVE	51
ACTIVITY 2.15	PUTTING IT TOGETHER	53
CYLINDERS		**57**
ACTIVITY 3.1	DRAWING CIRCLES & ELLIPSES	59
ACTIVITY 3.2	CYLINDER FROM DIVIDE-THE-BOX TECHNIQUE	61
ACTIVITY 3.3	CYLINDER OBJECTS FROM THE BOX	63
ACTIVITY 3.4	MULTI-ELLIPSE CYLINDERS	65
ACTIVITY 3.5	COMPLEX CYLINDER OBJECTS	67
ACTIVITY 3.6	CYLINDERS USING CENTER-LINE TECHNIQUE	69
ACTIVITY 3.7	PUTTING IT TOGETHER	71
TEXTURE & PATTERN		**73**
ACTIVITY 4.1	VALUE SCALES	75
ACTIVITY 4.2	IMPLIED TEXTURES	77
ACTIVITY 4.3	ACTUAL TEXTURE & SURFACE RENDERING	79
ACTIVITY 4.4	WOOD RENDERING	81

| ACTIVITY 4.5 | WOOD RENDERING ON AN OBJECT | 83 |
| ACTIVITY 4.6 | PUTTING IT TOGETHER | 85 |

SHADE & SHADOW 87

ACTIVITY 5.1	SHADE AND SHADOW WITH AN OPEN BOX	89
ACTIVITY 5.2	SHADE AND SHADOW WITH SHAPES	91
ACTIVITY 5.3	DEFINING CAST SHADOW	93
ACTIVITY 5.4	SHADE AND SHADOW ON AN OBJECT	95
ACTIVITY 5.5	SHADE AND SHADOW ON A BRICK BENCH	97
ACTIVITY 5.6	SHADE, SHADOW AND SHAPE ON A JAR	99
ACTIVITY 5.7	PUTTING IT TOGETHER	101

DRAWING PLANTS 103

ACTIVITY 6.1	DRAWING A LEAF	105
ACTIVITY 6.2	DRAWING A PLANT CONTAINER	107
ACTIVITY 6.3	ADDING PLANT TO CONTAINER	109
ACTIVITY 6.4	COMBINED PLANT AND CONTAINER	111
ACTIVITY 6.5	PUTTING IT TOGETHER	113

COMPOSITION 115

ACTIVITY 7.1	BALANCED COMPOSITION	117
ACTIVITY 7.2	COMPOSITION INTEREST	119
ACTIVITY 7.3	ADDING A FOCAL POINT	121
ACTIVITY 7.4	PUTTING IT TOGETHER	123

FURNITURE & ACCESSORIES 125

ACTIVITY 8.1	ONE-POINT PERSPECTIVE SIDE TABLE	127
ACTIVITY 8.2	ONE-POINT PERSPECTIVE OTTOMAN	129
ACTIVITY 8.3	ONE-POINT PERSPECTIVE SIDE CHAIR	133
ACTIVITY 8.4	RENDERING FABRIC PATTERN	135
ACTIVITY 8.5	TWO-POINT PERSPECTIVE SIDE TABLE	137
ACTIVITY 8.6	TWO-POINT PERSPECTIVE OTTOMAN	139
ACTIVITY 8.7	TWO-POINT PERSPECTIVE SIDE CHAIR	143
ACTIVITY 8.8	RENDERING AN UPHOLSTERED CHAIR	145
ACTIVITY 8.9	RENDERING ART WORK	147
ACTIVITY 8.10	DRAWING LAMPS	149
ACTIVITY 8.11	DRAWING BOOKS	151
ACTIVITY 8.12	DRAWING PICTURE FRAMES	153
ACTIVITY 8.13	DRAWING A LEONARDO DA VINCI PAGE	155

RECOMMENDED REFERENCES 159

Preface

This companion *Activity Sketch Book* provides a step-by-step approach for practicing and developing fundamental perspective line drawing techniques. I recommend having your *Exploring Perspective Hand Drawing* reference book available as you work through the activities; they correspond directly with the information in Chapters 1 - 8, which provides additional support material. In addition, a number of the enclosed activities have a corresponding video to demonstrate the techniques described in the reference book. These activities are denoted by a CD icon at the end of the instructions.

The collection of activities in this book is intended to provide a foundation for developing basic line drawing techniques. These skills are brought together in Chapters 9 and 10 of the reference book, where you will find instruction for creating complete interior design projects of one-point and two-point perspective rooms. For these projects you will be using drafting supplies and large sized paper; therefore, they are not included in the activity book. There are two additional video clips that demonstrate adding furniture blocks to a one-point grid and a two- point grid as support for these projects.

Some activities have examples of objects that I have drawn and yet you are asked to find your own object to use as a subject. Copying my image will not provide you with the same practice as drawing from an object in front of you. Also, I encourage you to adjust or change the activity to meet your own drawing needs.

Below is a quick list of the typical supplies and tools you will need to complete the activities. Please refer back to Chapter One of the reference book for more detailed information on using the tools.

BASIC DRAWING SUPPLIES

Drawing Pencils	HB, B & 2B wood drawing pencils one each
Eraser	White block eraser
Sharpener	Hand held, small pencil sharpener
Drawing Markers	Thin, medium, wide drawing markers in black or sepia
Eraser Shield	Small metal piece with holes used in erasing
"T" Square or ruler	12" small, plastic "T" square or ruler
Triangle	90 degree small drafting triangle

Below is a list of drafting supplies need to complete the one-point and two-point perspective projects outlined in Chapters 9 and 10 of the reference book.

BASIC DRAFTING TOOLS

Roll of Tracing Paper	Least expensive, white or yellow 24" wide tracing paper
Drafting Tape	Low adhesive drafting tape or dots
Architectural Scale	Triangular shaped or flat architectural scale
Triangle	An 8 inch or larger architectural triangle
T-square 36	Metal or wood 36 inch T square
Drafting Surface	Drafting surface large enough for a 24"X 36"paper
Velum Paper	Plain 24"X 30"velum paper

Chapter One

Orientation

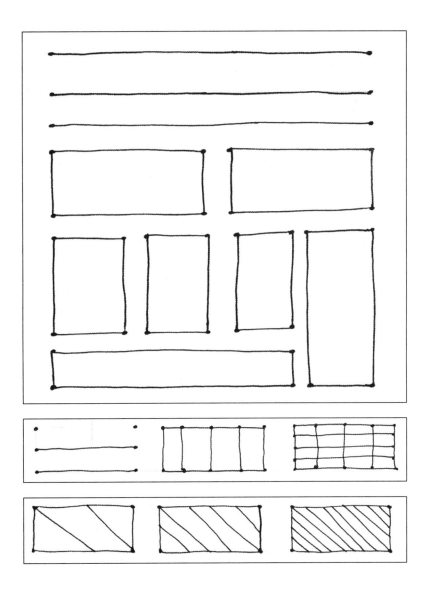

ACTIVITY 1.1   DRAWING CONSISTENT LINES

The use of guide points and guide lines is a helpful technique as you start to practice the skill of drawing. By anticipating where you want your line to go and placing a guide point at that spot, you can use this as a target for your pencil to move toward.

In this activity, plan to use the guide points below and practice drawing consistent lines (lines that are the same weight and thickness from start to finish).

❶ Using the points below, draw lines and box shapes that are similar to the drawing on the right.

❷ Put your pencil on the left point and draw a line to the right point.

❸ Let your eye move forward to the point on the right. Your hand will know where to go as you look ahead to the destination point.

❹ Repeat these steps to draw two more lines.

❺ Use the same point -to- point technique as you draw the rectangular shapes to finish the activity.

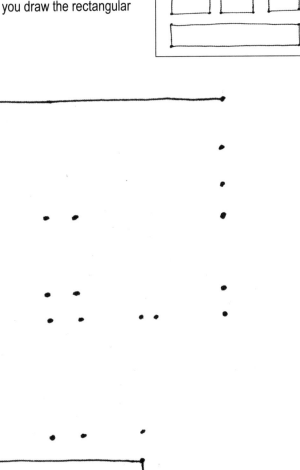

ACTIVITY 1.2   LINES WITH WEIGHT VARIATION

Practice the same technique of starting with your pencil on a point and moving it toward the next one. This time, practice drawing simple squares and rectangles and dividing them with lighter value lines. Vary your line weight by using a darker line for the contour of the box and a lighter line for the pattern.

❶ Using light pencil lines, draw six additional rectangular shapes that are the same size. Plan to use your T-square to assist with drawing these shapes.

❷ Darken the outside of the box shape and erase any extra guide lines.

❸ In each row, using a lighter line, reiterate the line pattern provided on the left.

❹ When adding the diagonal lines, start in the top left corner. Practice using your eye to draw each line an equal distant apart.

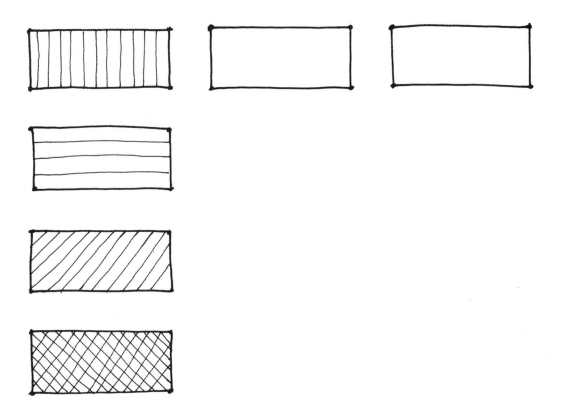

ACTIVITY 1.3   SQUARE BOXES WITH LINES

This activity is similar to the last one, except this time you will be adding horizontal, vertical and diagonal lines to a three dimensional box.

❶ In the first row, add lighter horizontal and vertical lines into the front square shapes. Repeat the pattern for the sides of the box and use additional lines to create a darker value. Notice the lines on the sides of the box and how the direction of the lines change.

❷ Repeat the same steps as above, only this time use diagonal lines in the square shape.

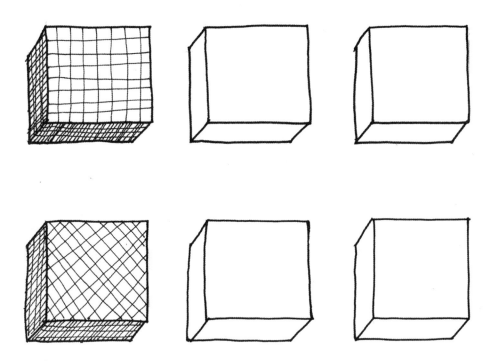

ACTIVITY 1.4   MORE PRACTICE WITH LINES AND SHAPES

This is your opportunity to continue to practice drawing consistent and variably weighted lines. Fill the page with simple shapes and boxes using different line weights. Use your T-square to assist with placement of guide dots and guidelines.

CHAPTER 2

The Box

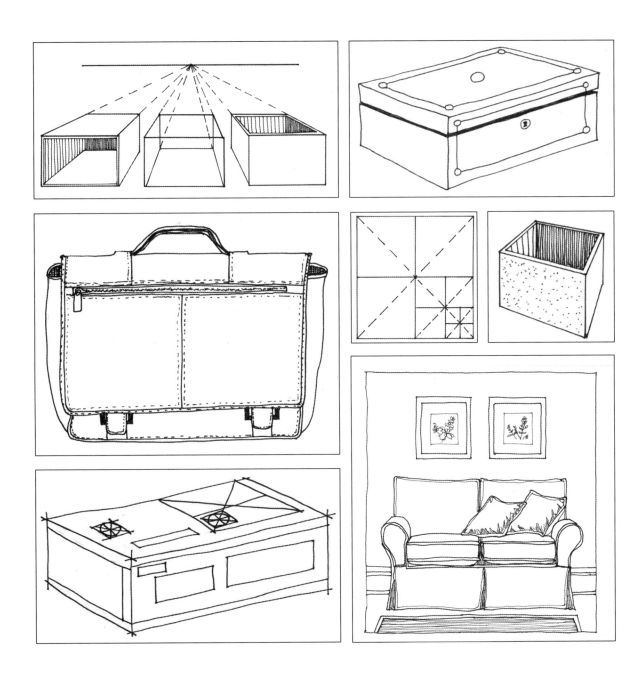

ACTIVITY 2.1   ONE-POINT PERSPECTIVE VIEWS

Use the drawing below to complete the one-point perspective box shape activity. The flat front of each box is provided as a starting point. You will add the rest of the box shape using the vanishing point. Your final drawing should match the example.

❶ In pencil, for each box, use your straight edge to extend the dashed perspective lines to connect the vanishing point to the flat front of the box. This will create the top and sides.

❷ Draw the back of the box with your straight edge, creating lines that will be parallel to the flat front. Darken the box lines.

❸ Define the inside of the box using two lines for the edge and a vertical line for the inside corner line. Add additional vertical lines on the inside of the boxes as shown in the example.

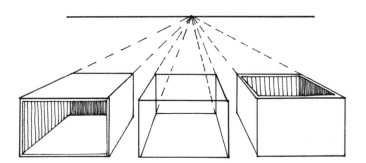

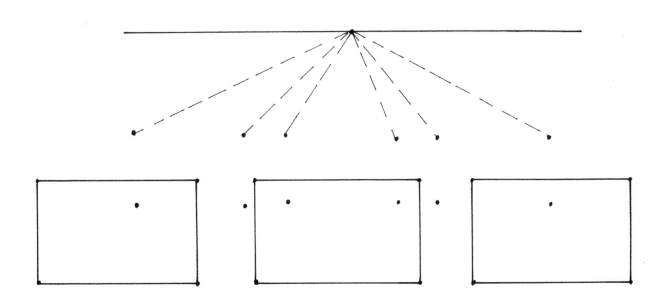

19

ACTIVITY 2.2　　　　　　　　　ONE-POINT PERSPECTIVE BOXES

In this activity, follow the steps below to add one-point perspective box shapes similar to the example.

❶ Start your first box shape above the horizon line provided below. Draw the box shape which represents the flat front of the box.

❷ With a straight edge, draw dash lines from the vanishing point to each corner of the box.

❸ Determine the depth of the box and then add parallel lines to define the back of the box.

❹ Redraw the lines of the box to darken and to make a distinction between solid lines and dashed lines.

❺ Repeat these steps, adding another box below the horizon line and another on the horizon line.

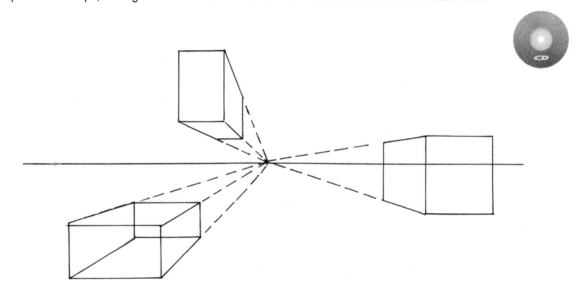

ACTIVITY 2.3   MORE ONE-POINT PERSPECTIVE BOXES

This activity is similar to Activity 2.2, however, this time draw your own horizon line with boxes above and below as shown in the example. Use the blank space on the next page for your drawing.

❶ Before starting your drawing, add guidelines to the drawing below using your straight edge. These guide lines should extend from the vanishing point to every corner of the box. Notice how the angle for the sides of a one-point perspective box always comes from the single vanishing point.

❷ On the next page, start your drawing with a horizontal line across the middle of the page and then mark the vanishing point in the center of the line.

❸ Draw a flat front box above the horizon line.

❹ With your straight edge, draw dashed perspective guide lines from the vanishing point to the corners of the flat front box.

❺ Determine the depth of your box and add lines that are parallel to the top and side edges of the flat front box to define the far end of the box. Darken the contour of the completed box shape.

❻ Continue to add more boxes from different positions above, below, and on the horizon line. Remember to always start each box with the flat front.

❼ Draw the inside view of several box shapes.

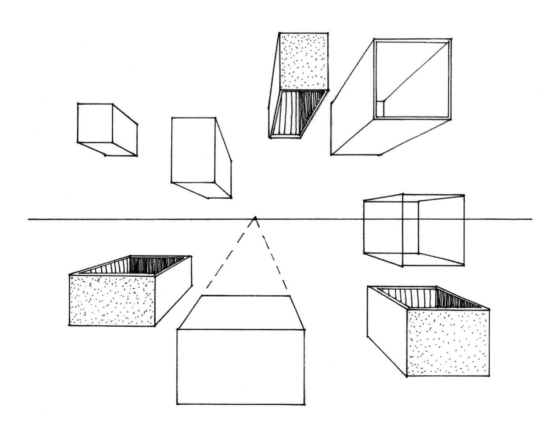

ACTIVITY 2.3   MORE ONE-POINT PERSPECTIVE BOXES

ACTIVITY 2.4   FREE HAND ONE-POINT PERSPECTIVE BOXES

Replicate the box shape three times using the space provided on the right. Do this activity freehand (i.e. without using a straight edge).

❶ Start each drawing with the rectangular flat front shape and add the details.

❷ For each shape, plan to draw the first two drawings with your pencil and the last drawing with your drawing marker.

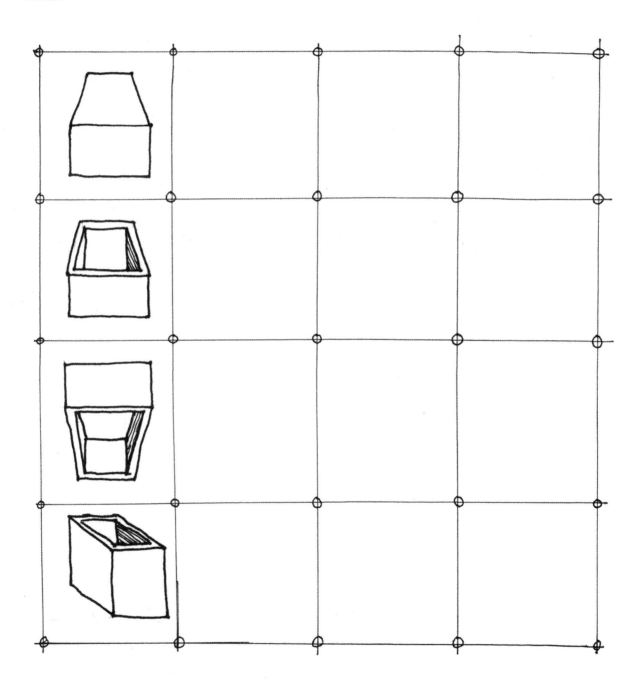

28

ACTIVITY 2.5   OBJECTS IN ONE-POINT PERSPECTIVE

For this activity, start by finding a simple rectangular shaped object to look at and draw. Face the object so there is a flat front. Look carefully at the proportions and the details. Taking time to notice the details of your subject is an important step for creating successful drawings.

❶ In the space below, start your drawing with a rectangular box shape. Plan to make the flat front shape at least 2 or 3 inches wide. Use your straight edge tool for the first 4 steps.

❷ Mark a single vanishing point at the top of your page.

❸ From the corner of your flat front shape, draw the top perspective lines angled toward that single vanishing point. These lines form the top side of your object.

❹ Use your eye to determine the depth of your object and draw a line parallel to the top line of your box. This defines to back edge.

❺ Plan to draw the details of your object free hand and without the straight edge tool.

29

ACTIVITY 2.6 TWO-POINT PERSPECTIVE BOX

These next four activities focus on two-point perspective. Use the drawings below and on the next page to draw two-point perspective boxes. Notice in the example with the numbers that the two vanishing points are off the page.

❶ Start with a line connecting points 1 & 2 to form the leading edge of the box.

❷ From points 3 to 4, draw a line parallel to the leading edge. Do the same from points 5 to 6. These lines define the back edges of the box.

❸ Darken the perspective lines between 1 & 3, 2 & 4, 5 & 1, 6 & 2 to complete the right and left sides of your box. Notice that the top and bottom perspective lines are coming from the left and right vanishing points that are off the page.

❹ Use the left vanishing point to draw a line from 7 to 3 and 8 to 4.

❺ Use the right vanishing point to draw a line from 7 to 5 and 8 to 6.

❻ Continue on the next page and repeat these steps.

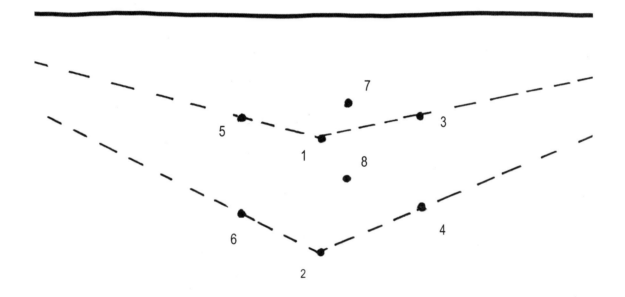

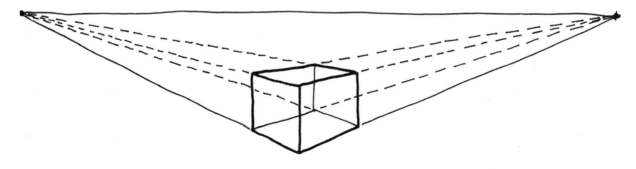

31

ACTIVITY 2.6 TWO-POINT PERSPECTIVE BOX

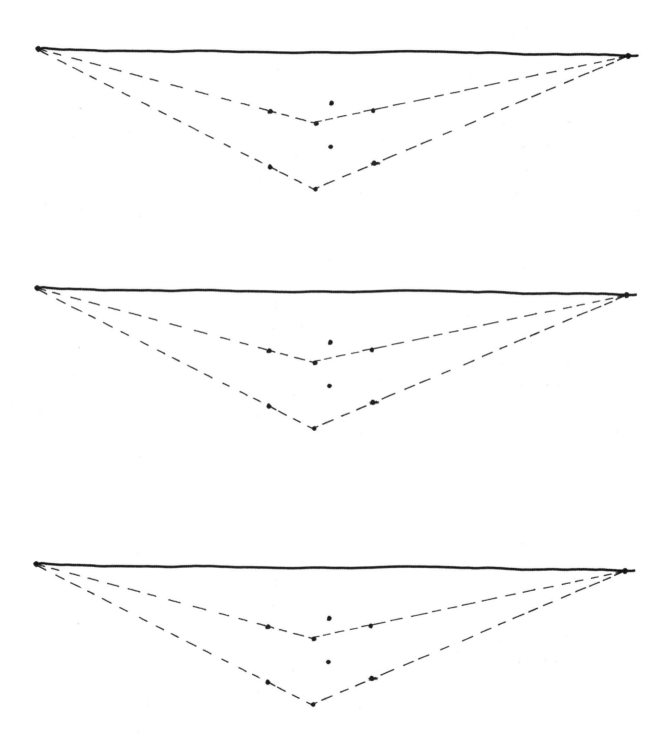

34

ACTIVITY 2.7   BOXES FROM DIFFERENT VIEWPOINTS

In this activity you will be drawing two-point perspective boxes from different viewpoints. Each box starts with a leading edge, perspective lines come from the vanishing points, and vertical lines are parallel to the leading edge.

❶ Before starting your own drawing, add guidelines to the drawing below using your straight edge. Add the guide lines from the vanishing point to each box. Notice each box has a leading edge and the angle lines for the side of the box comes from a vanishing point.

❷ On the next page, turn your book horizontally, draw the horizon line at the top and add vanishing points on each end.

❸ Draw your own boxes by starting with a leading edge. Use your straight edge tool to make the guide lines from the vanishing points.

❹ Use perspective guide lines to draw the top and bottom lines.

❺ Use parallel lines to finish the sides of the box.

❻ Draw boxes below, above and on the horizon line.

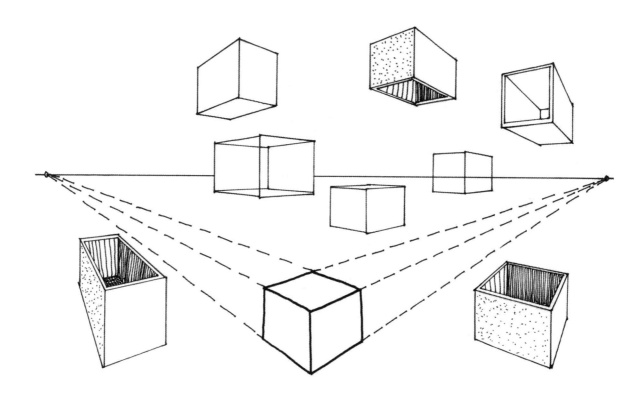

35

ACTIVITY 2.7   BOXES FROM DIFFERENT VIEW POINTS

38

ACTIVITY 2.8 FREE HAND TWO-POINT PERSPECTIVE DRAWINGS

For this activity, draw the box shape in the space provided on the right using a free hand technique (i.e. without using a straight edge).

❶ Start each drawing with the leading edge line. Add perspective lines using imaginary vanishing points. Add the other box details as shown in the example.

❷ For each shape, plan to draw the first two drawings with your pencil and the last drawing with your drawing marker.

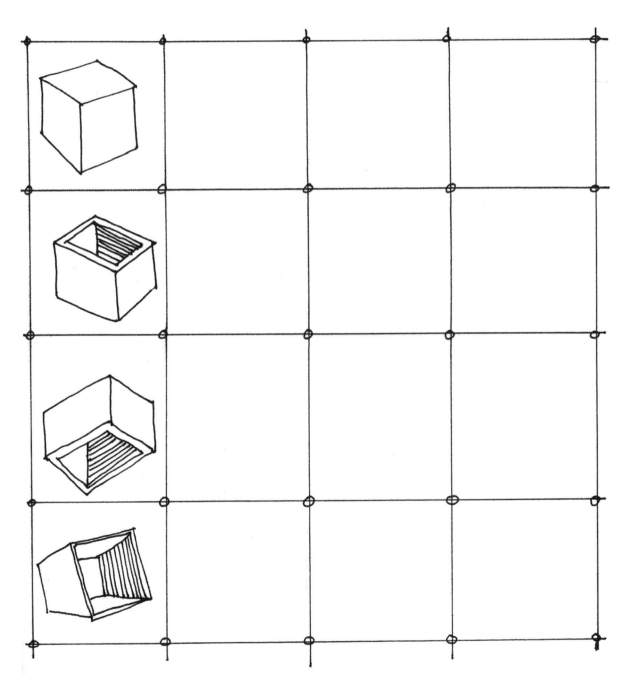

39

ACTIVITY 2.9   MULTIVIEW DRAWINGS OF OBJECTS

For this activity practice drawing multiview drawings of objects. In the space to the right of the object, draw the top, side and front views of the box and chair. Refer to Chapter 2 in the reference book more information on multiview drawings.

❶ Start with the box shape for each drawing. Plan to use your straight edge.

❷ Add the detail lines found on each object.

❸ Under each drawing add a label identifying the view.

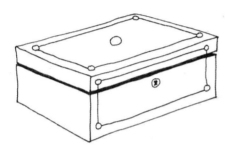

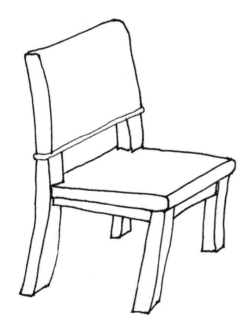

41

42

ACTIVITY 2.10   MULTIVIEW DRAWINGS OF SHAPES

In this activity, redraw the views of each shape to the right of the example. Notice the top, side and front views are flat without showing the shape dimension.

In the last diagram, dashed lines represent hidden lines that are inside the shape. These dashed lines represent edges that are not visible from this view.

❶ Start by measuring the shapes and plan to draw them approximately the same size.

❷ With pencil, using guide points and a straight edge as needed.

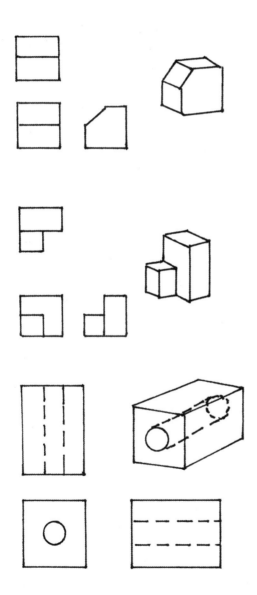

ACTIVITY 2.11 VISUALIZING THREE DIMENSIONAL OBJECTS

In the drawings below, there are three sets of shapes represented by two-dimensional multiview drawings. Draw the three dimensional paraline shape represented by the multiview diagram on the left.

❶ Start by measuring the shapes and plan to draw your three dimensional drawing approximately the same size.

❷ With pencil, draw the shapes and use guide points and a straight edge as needed.

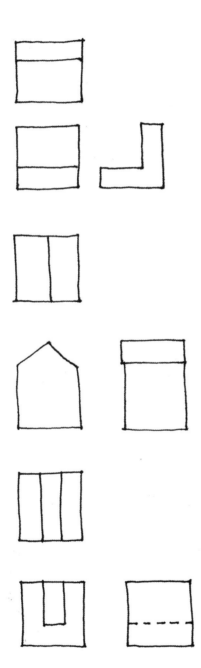

45

46

ACTIVITY 2.12   FINDING PROPORTION WITH A GRID

One technique for determining proportion is to start with a grid that is divided into equal parts. This allows you to focus on a portion of the object detail and to notice the relationship of shapes to each other.

In this activity, use the picture of the match box top as a guide to practice the divide-the-square technique for finding proportion. Draw the image of the match box top using the steps and examples as a guide:

❶ Measure the image and use this as a guide for your drawing. Draw your box shape twice as big as the actual image and using the same proportions.

❷ Using light pencil lines, divide your rectangle into equal divisions. Start by drawing a cross from corner-to-corner to find the center. Then divide the box into quarters by drawing a cross through the middle. Continue to divide each new square in this same manner.

❸ Notice how the divided rectangles are used as a proportion guide for the shapes on the match box top. Lightly add the basic shapes of the image to your grid.

❹ Using your marker, added your final lines and details. Erase any visible pencil markings.

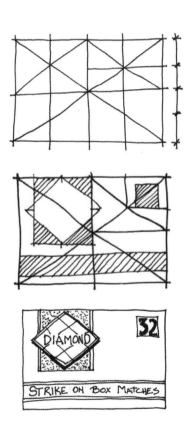

47

ACTIVITY 2.13　　　　　　　　　　　DRAWING A SOFA WITH A GRID

In this activity, using the box and outline below, draw the image of the sofa, pillows and pictures as seen in the drawing. On the outside of the box are lines providing 1/4th division of the box to use as a guide for placement of the objects. Plan to draw this free hand without the straight edge tool.

❶ Start by dividing the image to the right into equal parts by lightly drawing a pencil grid over the image.

❷ Use the rectangular shape drawn below for your drawing. Start by creating a pencil grid using the division marks on the side as a guide.

❸ Add details to the sofa outline using your marker.

❹ Continuing with your marker, add rendering of the two pictures.

❺ Add the pillows and the rug to your drawing using the grid as a guide for placement.

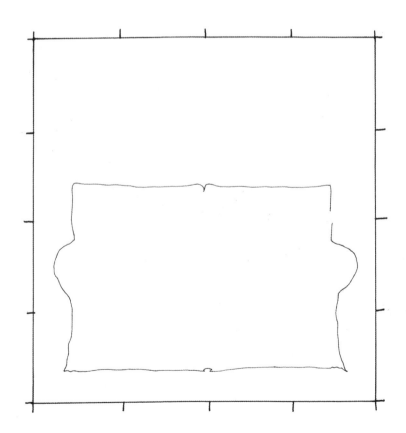

49

50

ACTIVITY 2.14   PROPOTION IN PERSPECTIVE

For this activity, use the horizon line and initial perspective lines to practice using divide-the-square technique in a perspective drawing. Plan to use a straight edge tool for this activity.

❶ Draw a square shape using the vanishing points to create your perspective lines.

❷ In this square shape, drawn an "X" from corner to corner.

❸ Draw a cross from side to side using the vanishing points and the center point of the "X" as guides.

❹ Repeat these steps to divide the square again.

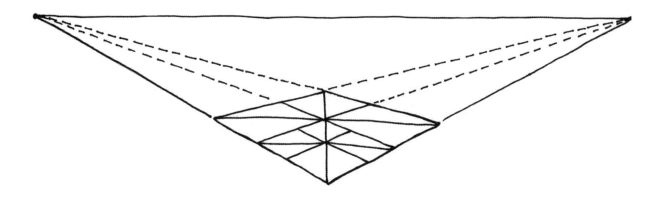

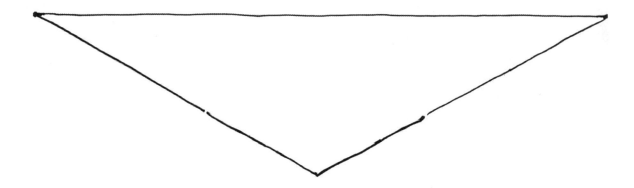

52

ACTIVITY 2.15 PUTTING IT TOGETHER

In this last activity you will be incorporating all the techniques from Chapter 2 using an everyday item of your choosing. Use the example drawn and the instructions to complete the activity on the next page. Here are a few ideas for objects that you could draw: tissue box, toaster, decorative box, tool box, jewelry box, phone book, frame, remote control or make-up compact.

❶ Find a simple everyday item and be sure it is a *rectangular* shape.

❷ Using your pencil, start your drawing as a simple 2-point perspective box. Remember to start with a leading edge and use your straight edge to draw perspective lines using "imaginary" vanishing points. Plan to have your drawing measure at least 2 or 3 inches in size.

❸ Add guide lines and shapes outlining the details of your item.

❹ After the outlines are drawn, use marker to redraw the contour shape. Then, erase any visible pencil lines.

❺ Add the details, textures and patterns to complete your drawing. Use your pencil to create guide lines or guide marks to aid with adding the details. You can alternate between pencil and markers and erase as you go.

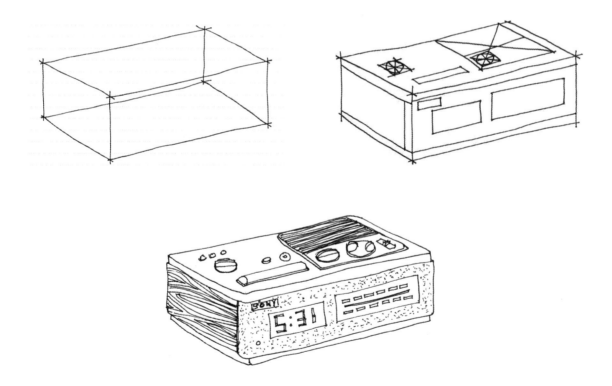

ACTIVITY 2.15   PUTTING IT TOGETHER

Chapter 3

Cylinders

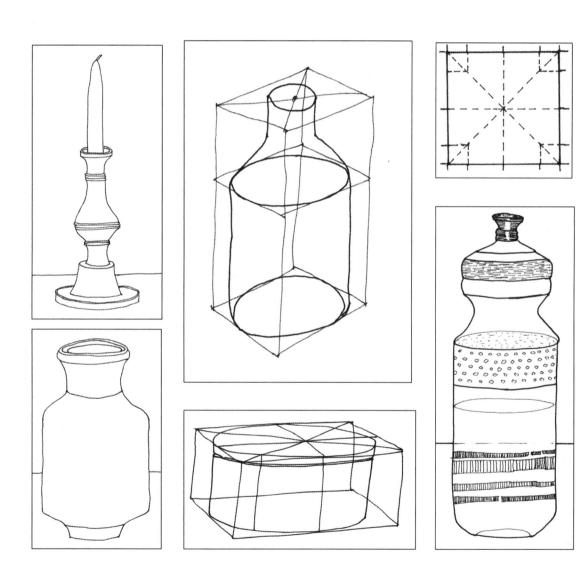

ACTIVITY 3.1   DRAWING CIRCLES & ELLIPSES

For this activity, use the box shapes below to practice the steps for drawing circles and ellipses. Refer to Chapter 3 of the reference book for further information. For each row, use the following instructions:

❶ Draw a diagonal line from each corner to create an "X".

❷ Draw a cross thru the center of the box to the edges.

❸ Create guide points by splitting each "X" into thirds and marking the outside third with a guide point.

❹ Mark a point at the end of each cross where it touches the box edge.

❺ Using the guide points created, draw curved lines from point to point to create the circle or ellipse.

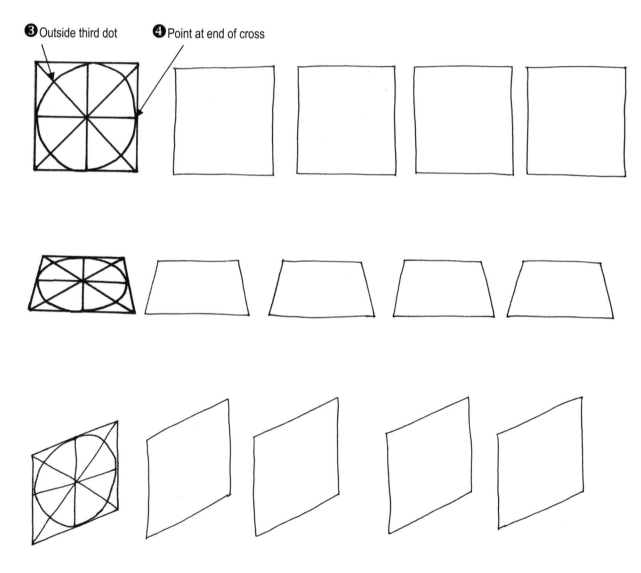

ACTIVITY 3.2 CYLINDER FROM DIVIDE-THE-BOX TECHNIQUE

In this activity we will expand upon the divide-the-box technique to create cylinders. Use the box shapes below and following instructions to draw cylinder shapes that are upright and on their sides.

❶ Using the technique from Activity 3.1, divide the top and bottom of the box with an "X" and a cross. Mark your guide points.

❷ Using the guide points, draw the top of the cylinder by drawing two curved lines.

❸ Draw the bottom of the cylinder by drawing only the portion of the curve that is visible from the front.

❹ Draw the sides of the cylinder by adding straight lines connecting the top and the bottom.

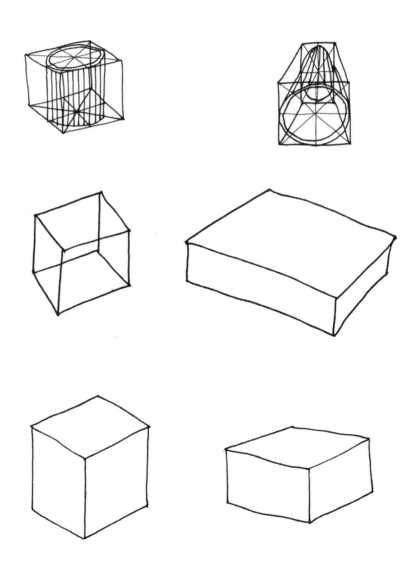

62

ACTIVITY 3.3   CYLINDER OBJECTS FROM THE BOX

This activity gives you an opportunity to continue practice drawing cylinder shaped objects. Use the drawing on the right as a guide.

❶ Start with one of the empty rectangular box shapes below and use guide lines to divide the top.

❷ Use the guidelines to add the elliptical shape on top.

❸ Draw the bottom, front edge of the cylinder by drawing a curved line that is parallel to the top edge.

❹ Extend vertical lines from the top to the bottom to form the sides.

❺ Use your drawing marker to outline the contour or outside shape of the container.

❻ Repeat this activity using the other empty box provided and then using your own boxes.

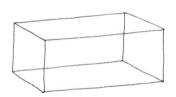 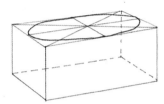 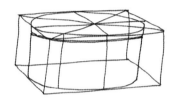

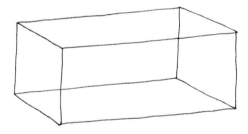 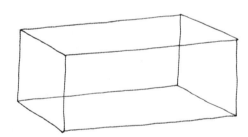

63

64

ACTIVITY 3.4   MULTI-ELLIPSE CYLINDERS

A water bottle is an example of a cylinder shaped object that contains multiple size cylinders. Use the three drawings provided as a guide and the rectangular shaped boxes below to draw a water bottle.

❶ Using your pencil, divide the first rectangular shape box on the top, in the middle and on the bottom.

❷ Draw the elliptical shapes for the top, middle and bottom.

❸ Use the edges of elliptical shapes as guides to add lines that will define the outside edge.

❹ With your marker, outline the bottle and add the label, water line and top details.

❺ Repeat this activity again using the second rectangular shaped box.

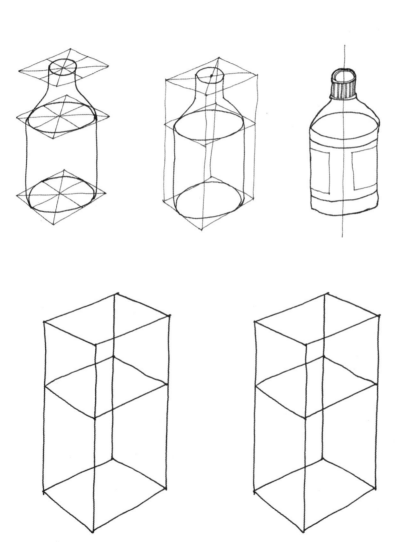

66

ACTIVITY 3.5 — COMPLEX CYLINDER OBJECTS

In this activity, plan to draw a mug in the space below. Use the two drawings provided and the example in Chapter 3 of the reference book as a guide. The first drawing demonstrates using guide lines to drawing the cylinder. The second drawing includes the handle of the mug. Here are the steps to follow:

❶ Start with a two-point perspective box and then divide the top with an "X" and a cross.

❷ Use these guide lines to complete your ellipse. Remember to draw two lines to form the top rim of the mug.

❸ Add a curved bottom parallel to the curved top.

❹ Start your handle with a side plane that is shaped like a backward "C". This plane is completely visible.

❺ Add the outside plane that is visible from the top and side, but moves under the handle toward the bottom.

❻ Add the inside plane, which can only be seen toward the top and toward the bottom.

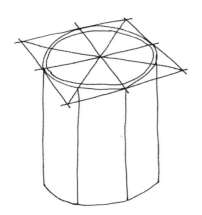
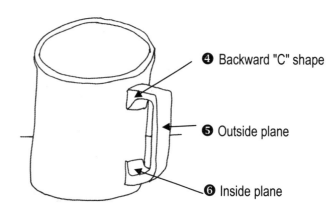

❹ Backward "C" shape
❺ Outside plane
❻ Inside plane

68

ACTIVITY 3.6   CYLINDERS USING CENTER-LINE TECHNIQUE

For this activity, use the two drawings below to practice the center-line technique when drawing a cylindrical object. Here are the steps to use:

❶ Finish the candle drawings below using the a center line and horizontal guide lines.

❷ Draw your own candle stick to the right of the drawing. Start by drawing a center line and then add the horizontal guide lines to assist with your drawing.

❸ Repeat these steps with the jar drawing.

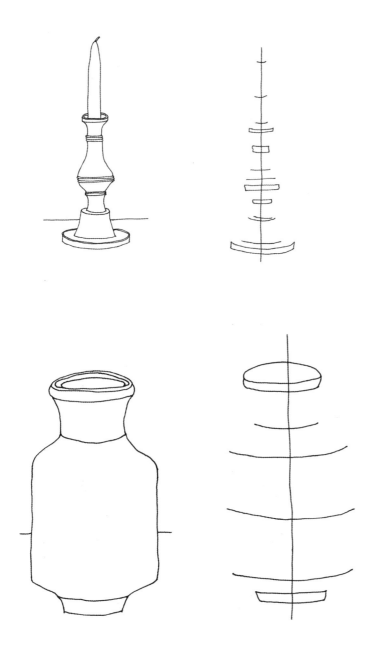

69

ACTIVITY 3.7   PUTTING IT TOGETHER

This activity provides an opportunity to practice drawing cylinder shaped objects using either of the two techniques covered in this chapter.

❶ Find two or three different cylinder shaped objects of your own to draw in the space below.

❷ Draw one of the objects using a rectangular box and divide the top and bottom for guide lines; or draw a center line and add guide lines to show the shape of the object. Use the drawing technique that is most comfortable for you.

❸ Plan to use your pencil as you draw guide lines. Finish your drawing with your markers, then erase pencil lines.

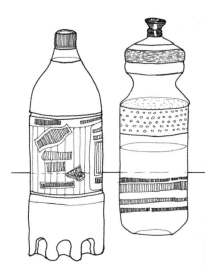

Chapter 4

Texture & Pattern

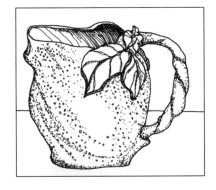
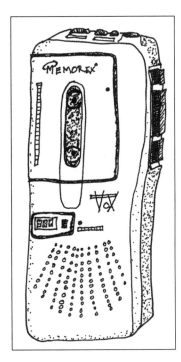

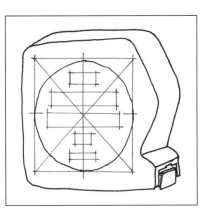

ACTIVITY 4.1   VALUE SCALES

To start this chapter of activities practice drawing value scales using three different rendering techniques. Use your drawing markers to complete this activity. Refer to chapter 4 of the reference book for additional information.

❶ Add three additional 1" squares per row, with 1/2" space between each square, to complete the three rows below. Use your small 12" plastic T-square as a tool to draw pencil guide lines for the squares and make them each the same size.

❷ Add gradated values to the inside of each square creating a value scale. Start with parallel lines in the first row, stippling in the second row and cross-hatching in the third row.

❸ Border the square with your thickest marker to complete the activity.

ACTIVITY 4.2   IMPLIED TEXTURES

For this activity, draw a variety of implied textures with your markers. Use this activity to experiment with different ways to render texture. These implied textures can be used as a reference for other activities as you add texture to your drawings.

❶ Add three additional 1" squares per row, with 1/2" space between each square, to complete the three rows below. Use your small 12" plastic T-square as a tool to draw pencil guide lines for the squares, making them each the same size.

❷ Fill each new square with a rendered implied texture using your drawing marker.

❸ Border the square with your thickest marker.

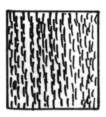

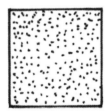

78

ACTIVITY 4.3   ACTUAL TEXTURE & SURFACE RENDERING

This activity is similar to the previous except this time you will be drawing a variety of actual textures. Take time before you start and gather samples of objects with textures that you would like to render. Render each texture three times to explore different rendering techniques. Refer back to these examples when looking for ways to add actual texture in your drawings.

❶ Add three additional 1" squares per row, with 1/2" space between each square, to complete the three rows below. Use your small 12" plastic T-square as a tool to draw pencil guide lines for the squares, making them each the same size.

❷ Using your drawing marker, fill each square with rendering of actual texture on an object or surface.

❸ Border the square with your marker.

ACTIVITY 4.4   WOOD RENDERING

Before you start this activity, find two or three different wood samples to view while drawing your wood renderings. Make an effort to have the characteristics of each wood pattern be unique. The sample drawings below are plastic laminate samples. The types of wood represented are river cherry, empire mahogany and limber maple. They demonstrate a variety of unique wood patterns and values.

❶ Draw, in marker, a rectangular box shape to render each of your wood samples. If you are using plastic laminate samples, you can put your sample right on the page and trace this shape.

❷ Look closely at each sample to discover the unique characteristics of each type of wood. Over-emphasize these characteristics and values. Make the darks darker and the lights lighter than what you actually see.

❸ Draw one of the examples shown and then add your own two or three wood samples to complete the assignment.

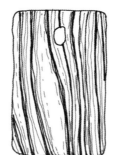  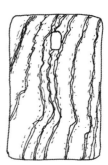

ACTIVITY 4.5   WOOD RENDERING ON AN OBJECT

For this activity find a rectangular shaped object made of wood that you can draw for this activity.

❶ Use your pencil to start your drawing.

❷ Draw the contour shape of the object in perspective and proportion.

❸ Use lines and dots to simulate the pattern and texture of wood.

❹ Over-emphasize the value and wood texture. Add as much interest as you can with the rendering of the wood.

❺ Add marker when you have completed the shape of your object and then erase the pencil guide lines.

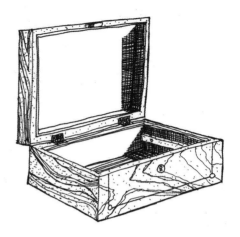

ACTIVITY 4.6　　　　　　　　　　　　　　　PUTTING IT TOGETHER

Here is an opportunity to take several objects with a variety of texture and pattern and combine them in a single drawing. Take time to find two or three objects that you can draw in the space below. Find both implied and actual textured in your objects.

❶ Use the same drawing techniques covered in this chapter.

❷ Using your pencil, draw a rectangular box and divide the top and bottom for guide lines using pencil. Or, draw a center line and add guide lines to show the shape of the object.

❸ Continue to use pencil for the guide lines depicting the details of your objects.

❹ Finish your drawing in marker and erase your guide lines.

86

Chapter 5

Shade & Shadow

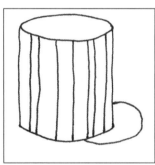

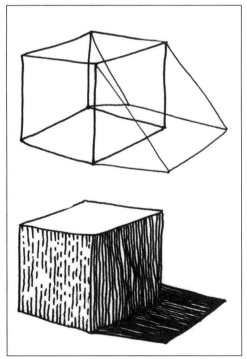
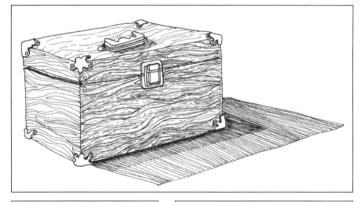

ACTIVITY 5.1 SHADE AND SHADOW WITH AN OPEN BOX

For this activity use the large box drawing below to add shade and shadow as shown in the example on the right. Here are the steps to follow:

❶ Keep the right side of the box white.

❷ For the inside of the box, using vertical lines, add a darker value on the right and lighter value to the left.

❸ On the outer left side of the box, using pencil, add two light horizontal guide lines, parallel to the top, which will be guidelines for value change. The first line will be half way and the second line will be one quarter the way up from the bottom.

❹ For the gradation on the left side, start with lines from top to bottom that have space in between.

❺ Add lines in between that are half way up the box.

❻ Add lines in between again that are a quarter of the way up the box.

❼ Use cross hatching for the shadow and make this the darkest value. Parallel the lines in the shadow with the outside contour lines.

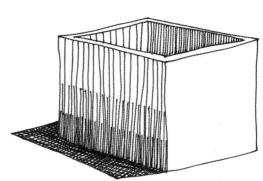

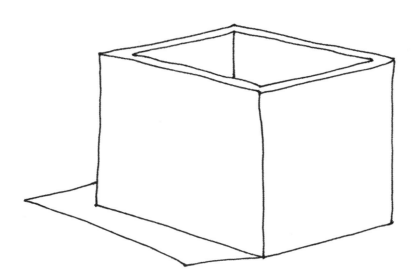

ACTIVITY 5.2   SHADE AND SHADOW WITH SHAPES

In this activity you will be adding shade and shadow to geometric shapes. Use the example in Chapter 5 of the reference book as a guide.

❶ Start by drawing two additional shapes that match each shape shown. Use your pencil first and then add marker to the contour of the shapes.

❷ For each of the shapes you added, use your pencil to draw dividing lines where the value changes.

❸ For the first shape, use your marker to add gradated value using <u>stippling</u>. Do this for the shading and the shadow.

❹ For the second shape, again use your marker to add gradated value, except this time use <u>lines</u> to create shade and shadow.

❺ Erase any pencil lines.

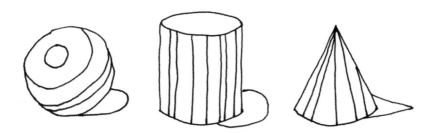

92

ACTIVITY 5.3 　　　　　　　　　　　DEFINING CAST SHADOW

For this activity, practice adding a cast shadow to a box. Use the shadow example on the right that demonstrates a single light source and two-point perspective guide lines to find the shadow shape on the ground.

❶ Use a straight edge and connect the sun to each corner of the box, continuing the dotted lines. These dotted lines represent a beam of light.

❷ Add a dark shadow value to the shadow shape on the ground.

❸ Use parallel lines to the shadow angles with your cross hatching.

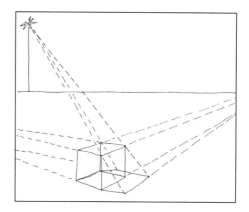

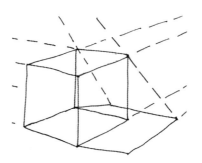

94

ACTIVITY 5.4   SHADE AND SHADOW ON AN OBJECT

Find a simple box shaped item that you can draw, similar to the bird house shown. Set up your object with a light source to the right front corner of the box. Darken the rest of the room so you can see the shadow.

❶ In the space below, start your drawing with a pencil outline of the object.

❷ Look closely at the values on each plane and the shape of the shadow on the ground.

❸ When you are satisfied with your pencil drawing of the object, using your markers to draw on top of your pencil drawing.

❹ Add the different shade values using vertical lines.

❺ To render the shadow value, use cross-hatching to create the darkest value.

ACTIVITY 5.5　　　SHADE AND SHADOW ON A BRICK BENCH

Use the photograph and rendered drawing of the brick bench to draw this same image in the space below.

❶ Start with your pencil to draw the brick bench shape.

❷ Add the shadow shape.

❸ Finalize the drawing in marker.

❹ Take time to render the bricks. Notice the dots are clustered at the edge of each brick leaving the center with a lighter value. Notice how the left side has more value in the rendering since this side of the brick bench is darker.

ACTIVITY 5.6   SHADE, SHADOW AND SHAPE ON A JAR

Here is an opportunity to practice adding shade and shadow to a cylindrical object. Use the jar container drawings below to add shade and shadow with your drawing markers.

❶ In the first jar, add value with <u>stippling</u> to show shade and shadow.

❷ In another jar, add values with <u>lines</u> to show shade and shadow.

❸ In the last two, add value to the jar with your own chosen technique.

❹ Vary the direction of the light source in the last two drawings.

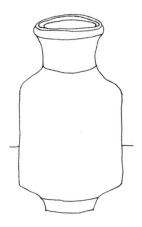
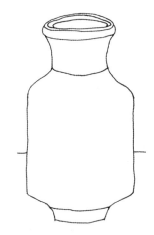
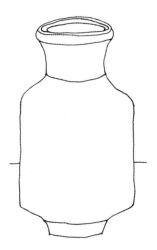
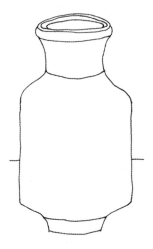

99

100

ACTIVITY 5.7   PUTTING IT TOGETHER

For this activity find several different shaped objects to draw. Set up your objects with a light source coming from the right and front. Darken the rest of the room.

❶ In the space below, start with pencil guide lines and finish your drawing with drawing markers.

❷ Use the same drawing techniques covered in the first five chapters to complete your drawing.

❸ Add rendering, varying your textures using line and stippling. Include values that range from white to very dark. This will provide contrast, which adds interest to your finished drawing.

101

Chapter 6
Drawing Plants

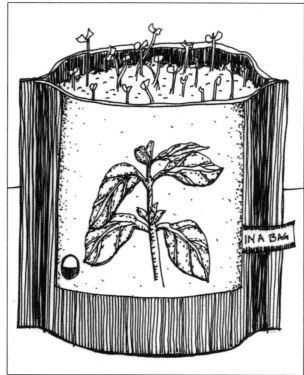

ACTIVITY 6.1   DRAWING A LEAF

For this activity you will focus on a single leaf. Take a leaf off of a plant and study its unique characteristics. You will be drawing this leaf three times, imitating the example shown. Start your drawing with pencil guide lines as needed and finish it with drawing markers.

❶ In the first drawing, use line to draw the contour of the leaf. Use two lines to add the veins on the inside of the leaf.

❷ In the second drawing, repeat the first drawing and add stippling for value and shape. Notice the stippling is clustered close the veins giving the leaf a curved shape.

❸ In the third drawing, repeat the steps of the first and second drawings. Add a rectangular shape behind the leaf and draw value with vertical lines.

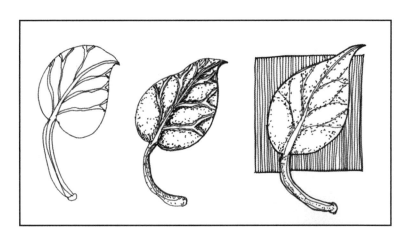

106

ACTIVITY 6.2   DRAWING A PLANT CONTAINER

This activity provides basic steps for creating a simple container, an integral part of indoor plants. The top drawing demonstrates how guide lines were used to develop the plant container. The bottom drawing shows the finished plant container. Plan to draw your container on the right side of the finished drawing. Here are the steps you can use.

❶ In pencil, start the container with a rectangular two-point perspective shape.

❷ Use the "X" and the cross from corner to corner to find the center. Draw a horizontal line through the center.

❸ Draw the rim of the container with two ellipses and using your guide lines.

❹ Add the top portion of the container by first drawing a rectangle beneath your rim. Notice that the vertical lines originate at the outer edge of the rim.

❺ Add another rectangle beneath the first to form the base of the container. Add vertical curved lines from the bottom of the top rectangle to the base of the second rectangle to define the sides of the container base.

❻ Add curved lines connecting the sides of both rectangles to form the curved front edges of the container.

❼ With your markers, draw the container contour lines and erase pencil guide lines.

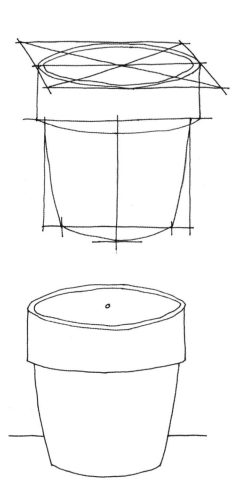

107

ACTIVITY 6.3 — ADDING PLANT TO CONTAINER

In this activity you will add a plant to the container. Use the container below and draw the orchid plant image shown on the right using the following steps.

❶ In marker, start in the center and add the two stems of the plant.

❷ Add the leaves.

❸ Add the pebbles and roots.

❹ Outline the container with your marker.

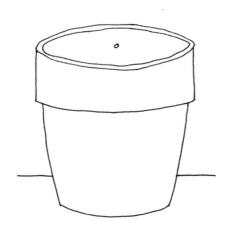

109

ACTIVITY 6.4   COMBINED PLANT AND CONTAINER

Before starting this activity, plan to find a live plant to draw. Take time to notice the unique characteristics and qualities of the plant. In the examples below, the first drawing is the pencil sketch providing an outline of the plant and container. In the second drawing, marker was added on top of the pencil drawing.

❶ Start in pencil to draw your container using the steps from Activity 6.2.

❷ Draw the plant with stems, and leaves as done in Activity 6.3

❸ Finish with your drawing marker.

❹ Using your straight edge, add a horizontal line representing the edge of a table.

❺ Add shade to the container and shadow to the ground.

112

ACTIVITY 6.5   PUTTING IT TOGETHER

This activity provides an opportunity to draw objects and plants together. Find several different shaped objects and a plant that you can arrange together.

❶ In the space below, start with pencil guide lines to draw the basic shapes of your objects. Continue to use your pencil until you are comfortable with your drawing.

❷ Finish the drawing with your marker. Erase the pencil guide lines.

114

Chapter 7

Composition

ACTIVITY 7.1   BALANCED COMPOSITION

Here is an opportunity to expand your drawing skills with thumbnail sketches while exploring the concepts of composition as outlined in Chapter 7 of the reference book.

For this activity, plan to have actual objects to look at while you are drawing. As you design your composition, there are several view points to consider. You may choose a close up view of a single object or a grouping of objects; or a broader view of an area of a room. Here are steps to complete this activity:

❶ Divide the space below into two equal size blocks.

❷ Use your drawing markers to draw a thumbnail sketch of your object.

❸ In the first sketch, find and arrange objects to draw an asymmetrically balanced image.

❹ In the second sketch, find and arrange objects to draw a symmetrically balanced image.

ACTIVITY 7.2 COMPOSITION INTEREST

Again, use thumbnail sketches to demonstrate principles of composition. Remember, these drawings are simple studies and not intended to be exact or precise. Have objects to look at for each drawing. For this activity:

❶ Divide the space below into two equal blocks.

❷ Plan to use your drawing markers to draw a thumbnail sketch.

❸ In the first sketch, find and arrange objects to draw that show overlap, contrast, and variety of shapes and textures.

❹ In the second sketch, find and arrange a single object that covers the space while leaving a small amount of negative space. Plan to incorporate a variety of textures in the rendering of your subject.

120

ACTIVITY 7.3   ADDING A FOCAL POINT

In this activity, have several objects with one that can be the focal point of your drawing. Refer back to the Chapter 7 of the reference book for different characteristics that you can use to add contrast, creating an emphasis on the focal point object.

❶ Start with arranging your objects. Be sure one object is larger or has other characteristics that will make it the focal point.

❷ In the space below, first sketch your drawing in pencil using rectangular box shapes and guide lines as needed.

❸ Finish your drawing with your markers and plan to erase the pencil lines.

122

ACTIVITY 7.4   PUTTING IT TOGETHER

In this activity take time to practice arranging a still life composition to draw. Have a variety of at least three different shapes when arranging your still life.

❶ Do a thumbnail sketch of your arrangement and use this sketch to review your composition.

❷ Move the object around until you have a successful composition based on the principles of design covered in Chapter 7 of your reference book. Notice that the example below shows a thumbnail sketch with three objects; notice how the final composition was changed. These changes provided more variety of shapes and better overlapping of the objects.

❸ Once you are satisfied with your composition, redraw your revised arrangement in light pencil. Add marker and erase the pencil lines.

❹ Complete your drawing by adding texture and value.

Chapter 8

Furniture & Accessories

ACTIVITY 8.1   ONE-POINT PERSPECTIVE SIDE TABLE

For this activity, use the illustration of the finished one-point perspective side table as a guide for completing your drawing. Use the started elevation to draw your one-point perspective table. Review the example in Chapter 8 as a reference of this activity.

❶ Start with your pencil and add the molding edge below the table top.

❷ Next, add the two stiles on the inside box, the top rail, and drawer rail.

❸ Refine the base shape using guide lines.

❹ Find the center of the drawer by drawing an "X" from corner to corner; then add the knob shape.

❺ Add a lightly drawn horizon line above the elevation drawing. It should be placed at a distance above the elevation that is the same height as the front of the elevation.

❻ Locate the center of the elevation and use this for the vanishing point on the horizon line. Draw the top perspective guide lines from the vanishing point to each corner of the elevation.

❼ Use half of the height of the elevation for the depth of the table top.

❽ Using your wide drawing marker pen, redraw the dresser outline right on top of the pencil. For the other lines, use a drawing marker with a smaller width. Erase remaining light pencil lines.

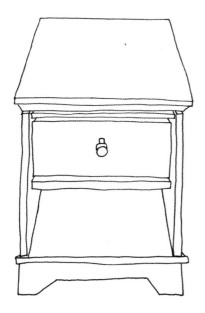
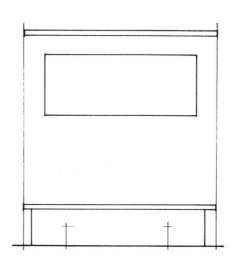

ACTIVITY 8.2 ONE-POINT PERSPECTIVE OTTOMAN

Use the example shown below for the first part of this activity and then use the next blank page for your drawing.

❶ Before starting your drawing, add guidelines to the drawing below using your straight edge. Add the guide lines from the vanishing point to the center of the row of buttons. Add guide lines from the vanishing point to the bottom and sides of the legs.

❷ Redraw the example below on the next page. Start by drawing a horizon line on the top of the page and placing a vanishing point in the center.

❸ Add the center ottoman first. Draw a flat front rectangle using your pencil, straight edge and T-square tools.

❹ Use the vanishing point to establish the top sides and then draw a horizontal line for the top back.

❺ Add rectangular flat front shapes for the feet, again using the vanishing point to find the properly angled lines for the feet.

❻ Use the vanishing point and horizontal lines to establish the location of the four corners for the buttons.

❼ Add the next two ottomans, again starting with a flat front rectangular shape to create the front.

❽ Use the same single vanishing point to establish the top, the side panel and the sides of the legs. Notice how the visible side panel changes with the position of the ottoman relative to the vanishing point.

❾ Add your drawing marker on top of the pencil to add detail and to complete the image.

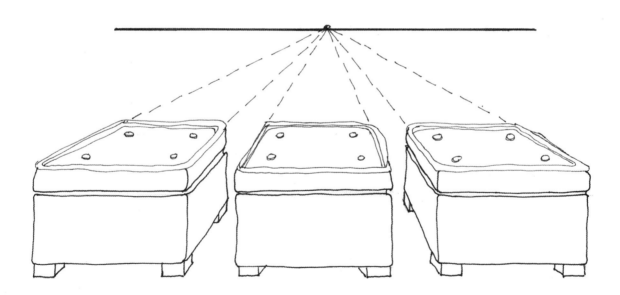

130

ACTIVITY 8.2   ONE-POINT PERSPECTIVE OTTOMAN

132

ACTIVITY 8.3   ONE-POINT PERSPECTIVE SIDE CHAIR

Before starting this activity, find a simple rectilinear chair to use as an example for your drawing.

❶ Start with very light pencil and draw a one-point box shape for the base. In the example, the back right leg and seat box shape were added.

❷ Add another thin box shape to form the back of the chair. In the example, the line for the fabric area was drawn.

❸ Using a darker pencil, refine the shape of the chair and add more details. In the second drawing, the curve in the back of the chair was added; the legs and base railing were added.

❹ To finish the drawing, use your markers to add contour lines and rendering.

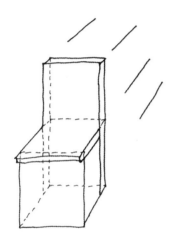  

133

134

ACTIVITY 8.4 RENDERING FABRIC PATTERN

Take time to select a fabric that you want to render on the ottoman. You can use an actual sample of a fabric or an image of a fabric design.

❶ Start by drawing the pattern in the square. You can lightly add pencil grid lines inside the square if this is helpful.

❷ Use the pattern drawn out on the grid as your guide for adding pattern to the ottoman.

❸ Add the pattern into the grid on the ottoman. Keep in mind that the further away the pattern is, the less detail you will need to add.

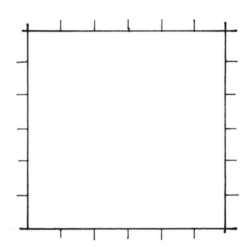

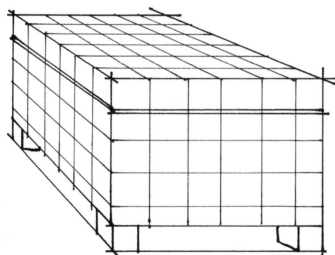

135

ACTIVITY 8.5   TWO-POINT PERSPECTIVE SIDE TABLE

For this activity, use the finished two-point perspective side table drawing on the right as a guide for completing the drawing below. Use chapter 8, Furniture Anatomy page as a reference for this activity. The center box shape is provided to start this activity.

❶ Start by adding the tabletop with the molding edge extending out from the center box shape.

❷ Next, add the fixed shelf, base rail and feet. Notice that the fixed shelf is wider than the center box, but the base rail and feet are the same width as the center box.

❸ Then divide the center box to create the drawer rail.

❹ Now the drawer perimeter lines and draw an X from corner to corner to find the center. Place the knob at the center of the X.

❺ Finish the drawing by adding end panel molding and the inside depth line of the shelf.

❻ Finally, add the books on the lower shelf.

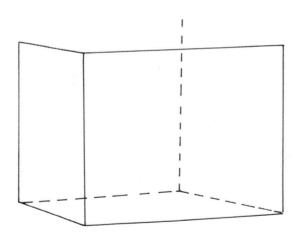

ACTIVITY 8.6   TWO-POINT PERSPECTIVE OTTOMAN

For the first part of this activity, use the ottoman drawing below. You will then draw the same two-point perspective ottoman using the next blank page; turn the book horizontally to provide extra space for the two vanishing points.

❶ Add guidelines to the drawing below with your straight edge. Add the guide lines from the vanishing point through the center of the row of buttons. Add guide lines from the vanishing point to the bottom left and right leg lines.

❷ On the next page, draw a horizontal line, across the whole page, and add two vanishing points on either end of the line.

❸ Start the ottoman drawing by first drawing the vertical leading edge line using your pencil. Plan to have this close to the bottom of the page.

❹ Use the vanishing points to establish the shape of the base, both the sides, and the top.

❺ Using the vanishing points, add double lines to define the cushion top.

❻ Add the feet below the base.

❼ Add piping to the top and use the guide lines from the vanishing point to properly position the buttons.

❽ Add your drawing marker on top of the pencil to complete the image.

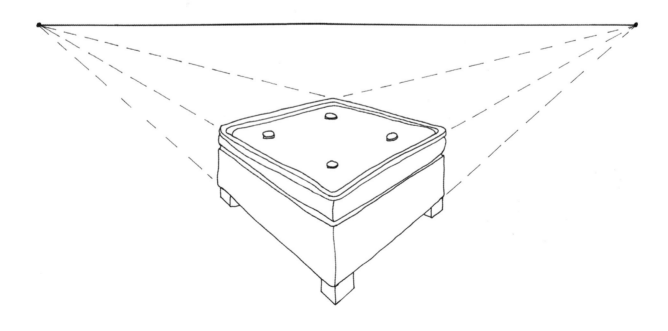

ACTIVITY 8.6　　　　　　　TWO-POINT PERSPECTIVE OTTOMAN

ACTIVITY 8.7 TWO-POINT PERSPECTIVE SIDE CHAIR

Before starting this activity, find a simple rectilinear chair to use as an example for your drawing.

❶ Start with very light pencil and draw a two-point box shape for the base. In the example, the back front leg and seat box shape were added.

❷ Add another thin box shape to form the back of the chair. In the example, the line for the fabric area was drawn.

❸ Using a darker pencil, refine the shape of the chair and add more details. In the second drawing, the curve in the back of the chair was added; the legs and base railing were added.

❹ To finish the drawing, use your markers to add contour lines and rendering.

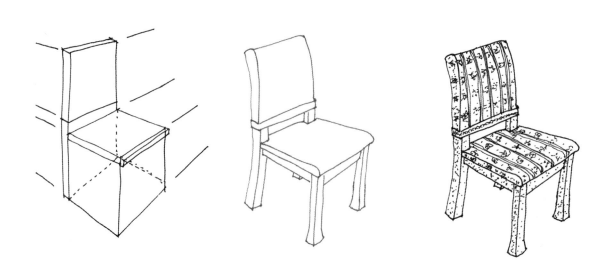

144

ACTIVITY 8.8　　　　　RENDERING AN UPHOLSTERED CHAIR

In this activity practice drawing and adding fabric patterns to a upholstered chair. Find two fabric patterns, either actual patterns or images of patterns to use for your drawings.

❶ Start by drawing each pattern in the squares provided. You can lightly add pencil grid lines inside the square if this is helpful.

❷ Use the pattern drawn out on the grid as your guide for adding the pattern to the chair.

❸ In the second chair, add the grid and your pattern.

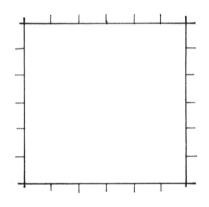
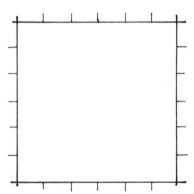

145

ACTIVITY 8.9　　　　　　　　　　　　　　　　　　　RENDERING ART WORK

This activity will give you an opportunity to practice rendering art work. Before starting, have four different pictures that you can use as a starting point for each drawing. The goal is to render each art piece in a subtle, suggested impression of the actual picture. Use the four frames below to draw your images. Here are techniques that you can use:

❶ Create an impression of the image with low values using your small nib drawing marker.

❷ Avoid using symbols which attract the eye and will create an over emphasized focal point. These shapes include circles, triangles, crosses or spirals.

❸ Avoid drawing large single objects such as a flower or a tree.

❹ Add a matte to several of your drawings. Add the depth for the matte on the top and right side.

ACTIVITY 8.10   DRAWING LAMPS

The goal of this activity is to practice drawing lamps with the correct proportion. For these drawings, use the center line technique covered in Chapter 3. Plan to redraw each lamp on the right side. Use the dimension lines as a guide for drawing the correct proportions.

❶ Start with pencil and draw the dimension line horizontally to the right side matching the example.

❷ Draw a center guide line for the middle of the lamp and use this plus the dimension line to define proportion.

❸ Draw vertical guide lines for the width of the lamp. Connect these lines to form the contour of the lamp.

❹ Add the remaining details then complete the drawing by adding your markers.

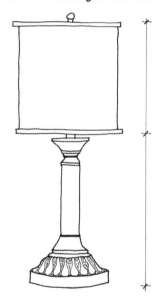

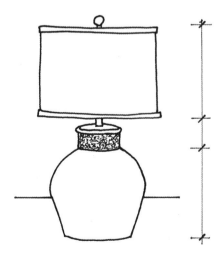

150

ACTIVITY 8.11   DRAWING BOOKS

Before you start this activity, find several books to draw in one-point perspective. Refer to the examples below as a guide for this activity. The first example shows the box shapes and perspective guidelines going to an imaginary single vanishing point. The second drawing shows the finished ink drawing.

❶ Use the empty space below to draw your books. In pencil, create the box shapes that outline the books.

❷ When you are satisfied with the shape and proportion of your book drawing, use your marker to refine them.

❸ Add double lines for the thickness of the cover, curve the binding area and block out the design of the book covers.

❹ Although it is not shown, you can add value, pattern and texture to your book drawing.

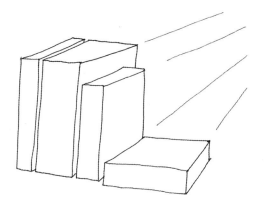

151

ACTIVITY 8.12 — DRAWING PICTURE FRAMES

For this activity, find a table top picture frame that you can use to draw in a two-point perspective. Position the frame with the left side as a leading edge. Use the drawing below as a guide.

❶ Start by drawing the rectangular front of the frame.

❷ Add an additional rectangle on the inside to form the molding lines. Create rendering of depth to the right side and bottom.

❸ Add the outside frame depth to the left side and the top. The visible depth will depend on the position of your frame.

❹ Notice that this example has two layers of molding. Look closely at your frame and any unique characteristics.

❺ Add a darker value to the sides of the frame to render shading.

❻ Add a rendered image.

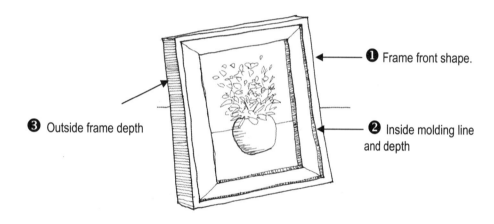

❸ Outside frame depth

❶ Frame front shape.

❷ Inside molding line and depth

154

ACTIVITY 8.13   DRAWING A LEONARDO DA VINCI PAGE

Drawing a series of the same subject is a way to improve your drawing skills. Your drawings will also improve as you become more familiar with a subject. In the sample below, I was practicing drawing different types and sizes of lamps. For this activity, plan to find a subject that you can draw multiple times to create what I call a Leonardo da Vinci page.

❶ Choose an object or subject that you are interested in practicing to draw.

❷ Plan to fill up the following practice page with multiple drawings of your subject. Composition is not being considered. Have some fun playing around with your drawings.

156

ACTIVITY 8.13   DRAWING A LEONARDO DA VINCI PAGE

158

Recommended References

Gerds, Donald A, *Perspective: A Step-By-Step Guide for Mastering Perspective by using a Grid System*, DAG DESIGH, 2002

Gordon, Robert Philip, *Perspective Drawing: A Designer's Method*, Fairchild Books

Hanks, Kurt *Rapid Viz, A New Method for the Rapid Visualization of Ideas.* California: William Kaufmann, Inc., 1980

Koenig, Peter A., *Design Graphics, Drawing Techniques for Design Professionals,* Pearson Hall, 2006

Laseau, Paul, *Freehand Sketching, an Introduction.* New York W.W. Norton, 2004

Mitton, Maureen, *Interior Design Visual Presentation, A Guide to Graphics, Models, and Presentation Techniques.* New York John Wiley & Sons, Inc. 2008

Montague, John, *Basic Perspective Drawing, A Visual Guide* New York John Wiley & Sons, Inc. 2005

Natale, Christopher, *Perspective for Drawing Interior Space*, Fairchild Books, 2011

Pile, John, Perspective *for Interior Designers, Simplified Techniques for Geometric and Freehand Drawing*, Watson-Guptill Publications, 1989

Wirtz, Diana Bennett, Hand Drafting for Interior Design, Fairchild Books, 2010